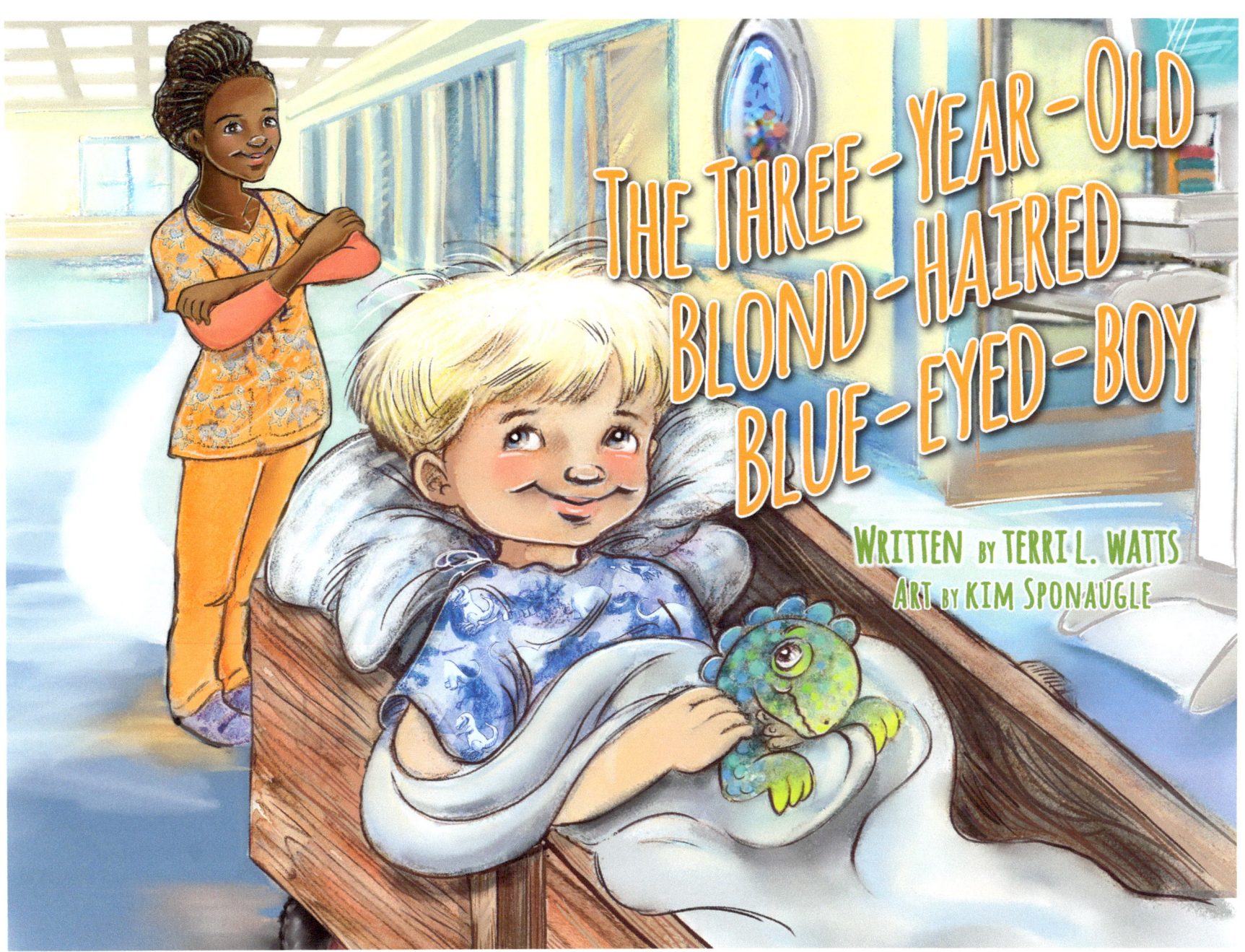

Disclaimer:
This is a work of nonfiction. No events are fabricated. The illustrated works of the characters, the dialogue to support the vision of the story and timeline, and the settings were based on real-life people (one being the author) and a specific place, not on the readers. The author and publisher decline all responsibility for any likeness drawn in this story from a reader's common perception or life experience that is coincidental.

The Three-Year-Old Blond-Haired Blue-Eyed-Boy
Written by Terri L. Watts
Illustrated by Kim Sponaugle
Book Design by Rosemarie Gillen
Edited by John Briggs

Copyright © 2023 by Terri L. Watts

No part of this publication may be reproduced, distributed, stored in a retrieval system or transmitted in any form or by any means, including photocopying, recording, or other electronic or mechanical methods, without the prior written permission of the publisher, except in the case of brief quotations embodied in critical reviews and certain other non-commercial uses permitted by copyright law.

FIRST EDITION

Paperback ISBN: 978-0-9666735-1-7
Library of Congress Control Number: 2023912503

Printed in the United States of America
Copyrighted Material
All Rights Reserved

Published by Vim Publications
Houston, Texas, U.S.A.

contact@vimbooks.com or visit
https://www.vimbooks.com
for additional information

VIM Books

Honor and praise to my Lord and Savior Jesus Christ
(Matthew 18:3-KJV)

Mama and Pappa, what fun, inspiring, God-fearing maternal grandparents you were!

Nana, thank you for believing in me and to Vim (Motherdear).
And two special fathers, one from birth and the other later in life.

Book Acknowledgment

Blessings to Kim Sponaugle, illustrator, and John Briggs, editor.
Thomas Moulder, The AdLab.

LeTony W. Hadnot Jr.
Different Mind Designs Photography

A blond-haired, blue-eyed boy lay emotionless in a dimly lit hospital room inside a secure steel crib.

As the nurse approached, his round head rippled dramatically.

His glare intimidated her. It made her feel timid and unwelcome.

His big blue eyes expressed a silent dread.

"Oh! What piercing blue eyes!" she thought.

He uttered not a word. Still, she assumed he loathed her in his perfectly shaped head as his haunting blue eyes followed her.

Don't touch me!

Deeply alarmed by his unpleasant contempt, her widening brown eyes could not hide her surprise.

"That's a bit much!" she said tepidly.

As his big blue eyes remained fixed on her, she cradled his arm to check his vital signs.

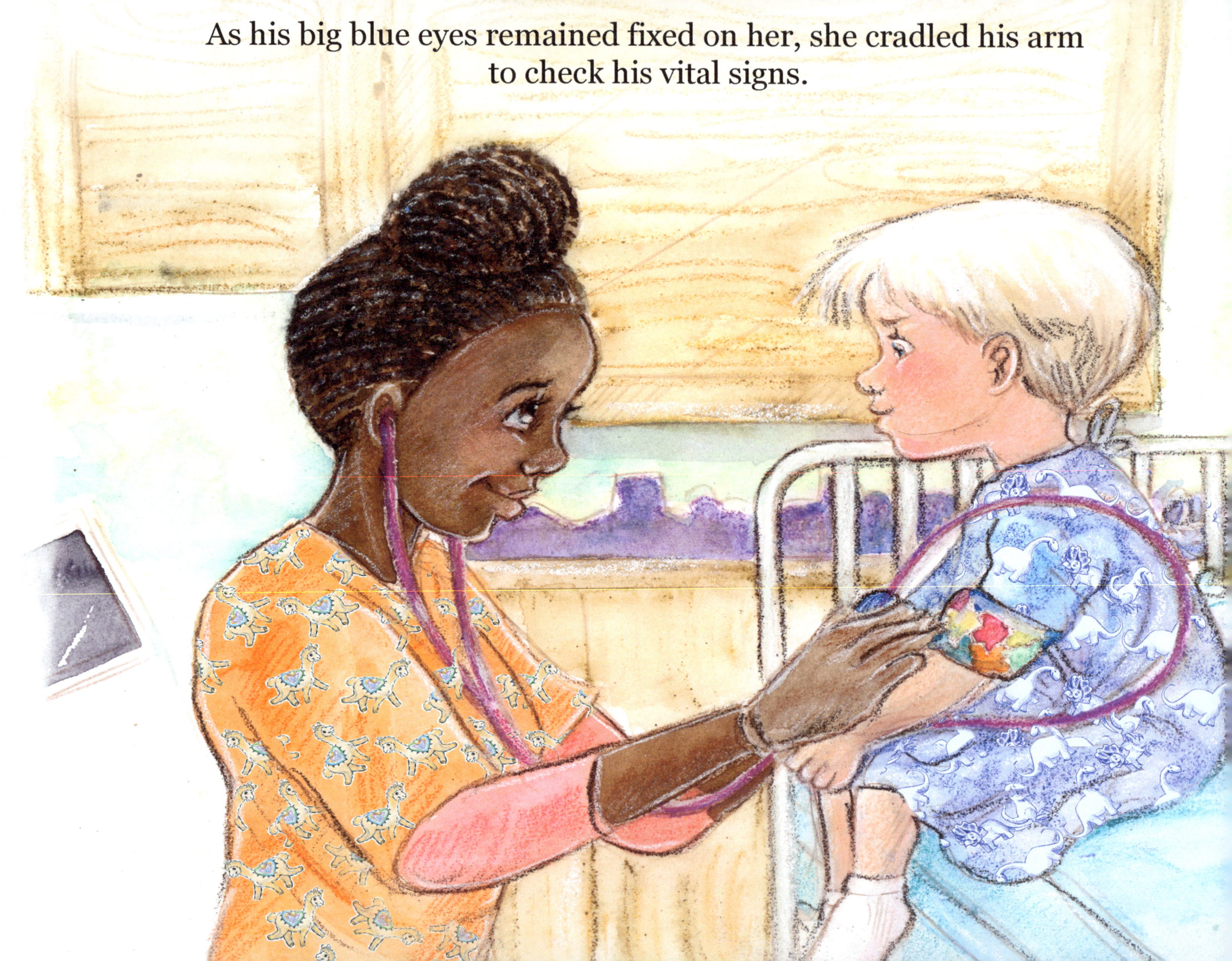

Once she finished, she hoped for an appreciative smile, but it did not come through. Instead, she noticed the mysterious effect his fierce stare had on his parents.

They laughed as if enjoying their son's self-righteous anger.

She walked out of his room, anxiously shaking as she reached the door.

He saw her no more until a quarter to three.

But when she returned, she brazenly lifted her squared and dimpled chin.

Yet, those brightly cresting, beautiful blue eyes that went on for days scowled at her once more. There was no mistaking it. He had an intimidating gaze.

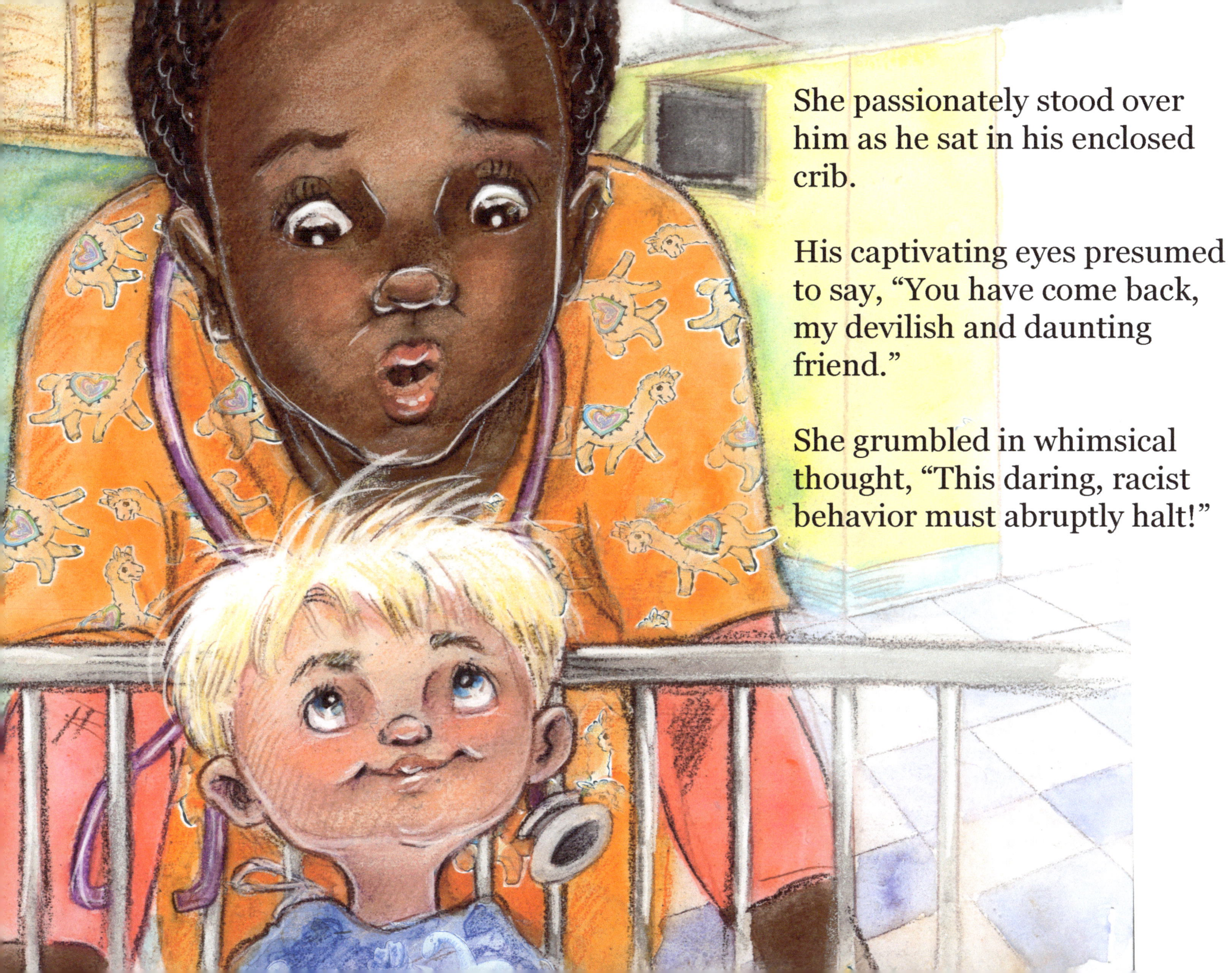

She passionately stood over him as he sat in his enclosed crib.

His captivating eyes presumed to say, "You have come back, my devilish and daunting friend."

She grumbled in whimsical thought, "This daring, racist behavior must abruptly halt!"

Once again, her hands shook. His artful blue eyes locked onto her temperament. She never felt such a rude awakening and sadly felt she had to accept his inappropriate behavior.

She turned away, believing she had failed to make a friend. The nurse could not understand what she had learned too late: "This blond-haired, blue-eyed, three-year-old child has been taught to hate!"

With her back to his face, her legs scurried her away.

But he laughed to no end as if to say, "Yes! I win again!"

Feeling depressed and defeated, the caring nurse paused and turned to his parents.

Again, they laughed as if enjoying their son's behavior.

Dad announced, "Oh, my friend, he loves you so much more than all the others who are about! Of all the doctors and nurses who have come in, he playfully singled you out."

The nurse turned toward her spirited patient. His gracious and controlled starlit eyes signaled, "Come near, my unrivaled friend."

For the moment, the nurse felt special. She wanted to leap over the sleeper sofa. She wanted to jump and to shout, **"Hallelujah!"**

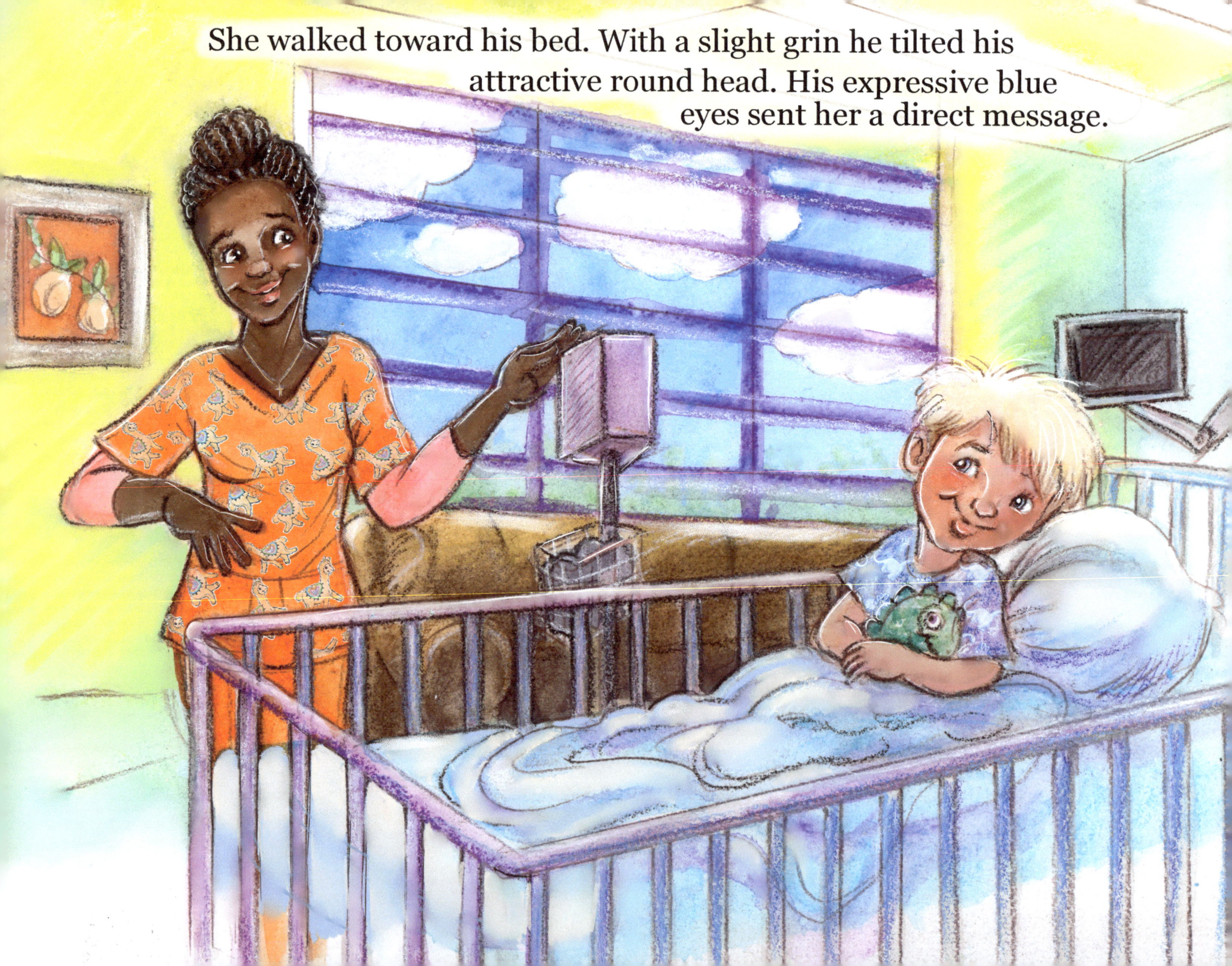

She walked toward his bed. With a slight grin he tilted his attractive round head. His expressive blue eyes sent her a direct message.

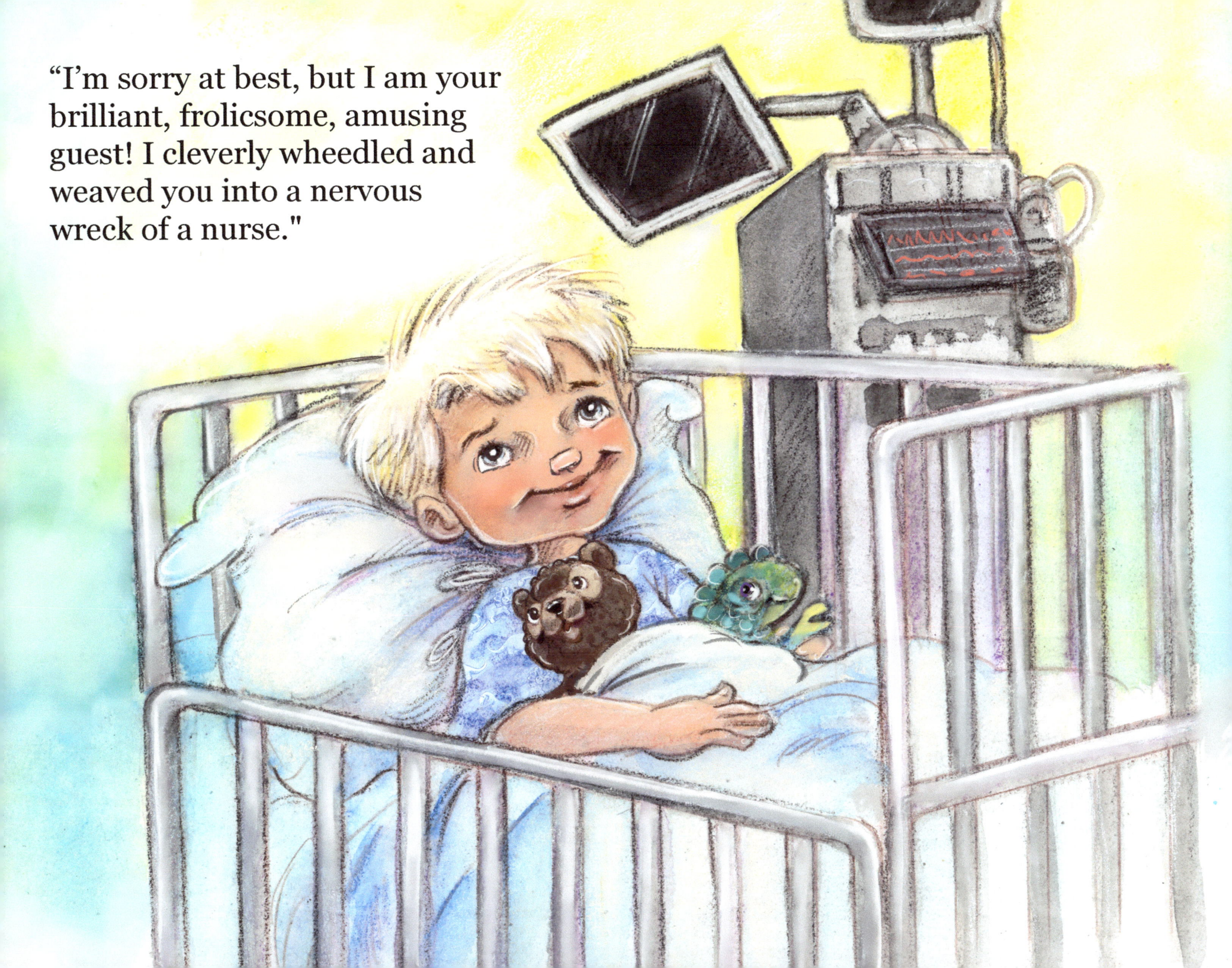

"I'm sorry at best, but I am your brilliant, frolicsome, amusing guest! I cleverly wheedled and weaved you into a nervous wreck of a nurse."

The nurse felt victorious that he was a doting and caring child. She gleefully walked toward the door after discovering she was cherished.

Once outside his door, he saw her no more. But she never forgot him and often thought, "Another gifted, three-year-old, golden-haired, blue-eyed, comedic pediatric will never intimidate me again!"

About the Author

Ms. Watts has a love for the Arts and World History. She earned a Bachelor of Science in Nursing with a minor in Biology from, Texas Woman's University-Houston Center.

She has spent many years working in the medical field as a registered nurse.

This is her first children's book. Ms. Watts has authored several Christian non-fiction books and is the playwright of the stage play *That's the Way of the World*, a romantic comedy and tragedy based on historical accounts.

She looks forward to producing a short film of *That's the Way of the World* and, one day, the screenplay, which made its way to the final round of competition in the 41st WorldFest-Houston International Film Festival.

She is the founder of Baby Llama Furniture, Inc.: Baby Llama on Board®.

www.ingramcontent.com/pod-product-compliance
Lightning Source LLC
Chambersburg PA
CBHW041326290426
44110CB00004B/156